Shadows
Of Life

A collection of poetry

NAZREEN

ISBN:-10: 93-5267-673-4
ISBN-13: 978-93-5267-673-6

Shadows

Of Life

Written by

Dr Nazreen

DEDICATION

For you

Contents

PART 1

MOTHER

High and low

I have searched

From end to end

Of this globe

And yet,

Not managed to find

A love *greater*

Than my mother's.

REPRESSED

Here I stay,

    Chained with a sigh

Despite my dreams

    That mount so high.

I see the butterflies

    Spread their wings and fly.

Why then are my wings,

    Doomed to die?

These binds rein me in

    From the sky,

Where I long to be

    If only I could try.

Whose egos am I feeding,

As here I lie?

With my fire

Left to dry.

BROKEN

When I think of you,

    There is no longer

    Any bright light.

No more any

    Crystal dreams

    Or petals milky white.

There is only an empty chill,

    The kind you feel

    On a deserted road at twilight.

LETTERS

I wish I could

Write your name

A thousand times

And a thousand more

On this piece of paper.

Write every letter,

Pour this utmost desire

Onto these alphabets

And scatter them high

Into the air

Till they descend

Like the rains that shower

Upon my heart.

PAIN

Wilted leaves have never

    Turned green again.

Fire has not ever re-sprung

    From an ash stain.

Then why won't you let go

    Of your pain?

WAVE

You were like

    An ocean wave;

After crashing in,

    The shores of

    My heart

Were never

    The same again.

TEMPORARY PEOPLE

I'm enough of an old soul

To know life is vast and deep.

I have seen enough to understand

Feelings come and go as they please.

But how can people reach

All the way inside till that

Little garden in your heart,

Plant blossoms and water them

Pull out the weeds and

Live there all summer

And *still*

Leave in the end?

HAPPINESS

Life is this

One big journey,

One great search.

You and me

And the rest of them

Are all knowingly or unknowingly

Seeking something personal,

Lost in this chaotic world.

Some chase wealth

And the rest power.

Some pursue their lost halves

And the rest their special dreams.

And then there is

You and me

And only a few of them

Who are drawn to a calling

We cannot make sense of.

But no matter,

No matter,

Because ultimately,

All of us

You and me and

The rest of them

Are all seeking

The same thing.

The elusive jewel

That evades all our efforts.

The one thing none of us

Can hold onto for long —

Happiness.

LABYRINTH

No one can discern

The chaos that swivel

In all of us.

The clutter of

Beautiful and terrible things

That lie scattered

In our psyche.

Is it not, therefore,

Both a blessing

And a curse

That they cannot see

The inside

Of our minds?

SECOND CHOICE

You come to me only

    After I wake up

    From my dreams.

My thoughts turn to you

    Only after all *else*

    Has fled from my mind.

The time kept aside for you

    Is the time I cannot

    Manage to kill nor fill.

Though you probably deserve better

    There is nothing more

    That I can offer.

WHOSE MISTAKE?

I do not deny

    The first to leave

    Was I.

It is true

    I did not wait

    To say goodbye.

I did walk out,

    Unable to stand

    This lie.

But since then

    I have always waited

    For a call that never came by.

GYPSY

Love is the only magic

    That can tame the

    Tempestuous oceans in her

    To calm waters.

Like a soft breeze,

    It will get past

    The flaming red of her hair

    All the way down

    To the wilderness

    In her little gypsy heart.

APPEARANCES

He says my

Eyes glimmer with

Stardust

And I dread the day

When he will realize

They are only

Ashes.

THE ONE

One day, like a snowflake

   On a mid-summer day

   She will suddenly appear.

Like vapours

   Out of the mist

   She will cloud your mind.

Then the dusty lamps

   In the temple of your heart

   Shall *finally* know fire.

UNANSWERED

I will always

Wonder why

I could not touch

Your heart.

Why we were

So close?

And *still*

So far apart.

DREAMWORLD

Each one us lives

In our own little

Dream-world,

Dreaming our own

Special little dreams.

And this is why

We cannot complain

When these fragile dreams

Take flight

To collide against

A reality we cannot

Comprehend,

And shatter into

A thousand fragments.

FIRE

You are the fire

That burns in me

With an

Unstoppable intensity

Even as I lie

Shivering,

In the frigid chill

Of this lonely

Winter night.

SEARCH

How sad

It is

That I continue

To seek you

In *all* my

Loves.

MIRAGE

You could be falling apart

With no will left to live,

Or even be too happy to sit in one place

With that exuberant happiness inside you

But the person next to you

Shall never notice the hurricanes

Raging in your world.

For what you see,

May not always be the truth

And what you think you know

May not always be real.

SUSPENDED

We are a discarded story, a confession that got stalled in mid-sentence.

Perhaps that is why, after all this time, I still hold onto to the idea of being in love with you.

FORSAKEN

Somewhere,

In one of the dustiest corners

Of my heart,

I have hidden away

The memory of you.

It stays there

So very quietly

As though hoping

The sun will

Shine upon it

One more time.

THE WANING

Slowly, I can sense it happening;

As your scent

 Dwindles from my clothes,

As the marigolds we planted together,

 Wilt away sadly

As dawns come and go so easily,

 Despite your absence—

The image of you that is steadily

 Fading from my memory.

CHAOS

Now writing does not free

These dreams within me.

Words do not drown out any

Of the music in my soul.

Pens give up and flee,

Failing to satiate this passion.

For my poetry had never failed me

Until I tried to write about you.

OPPOSITES

I grew up

And realized

That my

Love for you

Was true.

While you grew up

And realized

It was but

A game

For you.

STUCK

In this world

Constantly moving forwards

I am stuck

Looking backwards

Holding on to memories

That could not

Keep up their pace

With the rest

Of the world.

CHOOSE WISELY

There you are

Tethering on the brim,

Of giving up this fight,

Of succumbing to the walls

That seem to close in,

Despite your futile efforts

To keep them at bay.

But remember

If you give up now

You will spend

The rest of your life

Wondering what it

Would have been like

To choose the other road.

You will spend eternity

Questioning if you should have

Persevered until the end.

But this is life —

You don't always get

A second chance;

So choose wisely

While you

Still *can*.

UNSTABLE

How quickly but men forget!

    The fancies of the heart.

Like the honeybee that drifts

    From flower to flower

In the vain belief that happiness

    Lies on the other side of the field.

INCUBUS

On, the edge of a haunted wood

    Between the darkness and the light,

    Shrouded in shadow,

    He waits for me.

From heated hopes to feverish fancies

    In the midst of a mist

    Where one silhouette ends and another begins,

    I sense his longing.

Between the lines of reality and imagination

    Caress passionate winds beneath starry showers

    As the moonbeams fall to reveal

    The demon of my dreams.

SPACES

The unspoken thoughts

And forgotten words,

The incomplete sentences

And empty silences

Are just as

Important

As the things

We lend voice to.

STIGMA

Maybe if I stand

Close enough

To the fireplace

I can burn

In something

Besides this

Searing shame.

ACQUIESCENCE

I look into his eyes,

Still so deep and dark

After all these years.

Remembering the time, long ago

When I first fell for him

And all those times after that

When I fell again and again

For him.

But I can only cringe

And do nothing

Except return his smile

And walk away

Like all those times

He walked away from me.

THE OTHER WOMAN

I long for the day

When you will

Be able to look

Into the blue

Of my eyes

Without the silent hope

Of finding

Her

In them.

FORGIVENESS

We each learn

To forgive

Before we even know

What it means.

We forgave the toddlers

Who stole our toys.

We forgave the bullies

Who teased us to no end.

We forgave those people

Who walked out of our lives.

We forgave those dreams

That broke our heart.

We forgave those promises

Which were never fulfilled.

It is a heartbreakingly

Endless list.

But it is still

A long, long time

Before we learn

To forgive the most important

Person of all —

Ourselves.

HALVES

You and me

Are but

Two halves

Who tried

And failed

To create

A whole.

TEMPLE

Your body is *your* temple,

And like temples, it is

Beautifully sacred.

So cherish it,

Consecrate it

And claim it *back*

For in the end, it is the only home

That your wandering soul will ever know.

REGRETS

If I could, I would take it all away;

Every harsh word I did say.

If I could, I would ease the pain;

Every tear that you shed in vain.

If I could, if only I *could*,

I would heal the heart I so cruelly broke.

HEARTACHE

I see the shadow of a frail lily

Obscured behind your tender eyes

Just before you turn them

Away from my inquisitive gaze

Without answering the question

That remains unspoken in our midst.

And I cannot help

But wonder

How much longer

You will continue to pretend

That your feelings for me

Faded the day I chose *another*.

A PROMISE

I will find you again

In another life.

Kiss those fingers

In another body

And love you all over

With this *same* soul.

And for this alone,

I will be born again,

Again

And again

Until this lifetime

And all those lifetimes

That I lost you in

Will not

Matter anymore.

YOU ARE ENOUGH

Do not seek

    Your home

    In the hearts

    Of others.

There can be

    No home

    More enduring

    Than your own heart.

TIME AND SPACE

Just like the plant lived before the flower blossomed,

    And goes on living after it is plucked—

Just like the blank paper existed before the art appeared,

    And goes on existing after the ink has faded—

I was there before you entered my life,

    And I am here long after you have left it.

But it was a moment in time

That space which was filled,

Which made an entire life meaningful

For all of us,

And many like us.

ULTIMATE

I was not your first

And you were not my last.

But as the final stars are falling from the sky,

It is only *me* you will remember

And only *you*,

I will wish, was beside me.

NAZREEN

PART 2

WRITER'S REALM

Sometimes it gets so hard

To keep it all *in*;

The one million memories

That gush during lone moments,

The conflicts unresolved

That surface at the slightest touch.

What would I not do?

To be able to play,

Or to paint or to dance.

But here I am,

Having to pen it all down.

To write, write, write-

Write until the frenzy fades,

Write until the notes cease,

Write until the art blackens,

Write and write

Until I collapse exhausted onto

The paper that now carries

A portion of my soul.

HALTED

I wait by this rain-washed window

Playing a silent song heard by none

As springs come and years go

Whilst I yearn in solitude.

Though none has left

With a promise to return,

Though there is no one

Who would ever cross that road,

I wait by the window with

A flame flaming in my heart.

As I speak without speaking

Of lone nights, of yon lights

And hear without hearing

Empty murmurs that keep me awake.

But I keep waiting by this window

Left slightly open

Like a sliver of hope

Left waiting for *something*.

FORBIDDEN LOVE

An invisible mist has settled around me

With the whisper of an impossible love

Luring me on to a parlous path,

Even though none really exists.

But it is phantasmagoria I must close my eyes to

Like the moonlight at twilight

Weaving alpine flowers.

For it is but a wistful dream

That leaves me stranded in the middle of my heart

And lost, in the middle of nowhere

The red of the rainbow roving

In its unreachable core.

A rhythm I must dance subtly to

A tune I must never sing aloud

NAZREEN

A laconic poem I am doomed to whisper

A star best left radiating alone.

But the forbidden fruit has entered

Unbidden into my fickle heart

And though so close,

It is miles and miles apart.

LETTING GO

To watch as worlds shift

And our lives drift

Without a word, a sigh

Or a single spoken goodbye.

As he prepares to go away

And I take steps in the opposite way

Knowing he and I are parallel lines

Destined never to meet.

For I wrote our names in a heart

That worthlessly broke apart

When I could have written it in a circle lone

That would have gone on and on.

Although, I would have given worlds to stay,

Nothing did I say;

The past still kept aback

If only he were to ask it back.

So at these crossroads until we blur

He and I, further and further

Out of orbit, from things that *were*

Without *one last* word to spare.

RELAPSE

I sit huddled

With this terrifying silence

That crushes me

Behind closed doors.

Like ocean waves

They rush in and wreck me,

Dark and deadly

Across ominous shores.

The shattered glass fragments

Shine beautifully and terribly,

Weeping trickles of blood

Onto the floors.

And I finally know

What they mean by relapse

As the voices lead me to a razor

On all fours.

A BEAUTIFUL LIE

How true when they say to soothe,

'A beautiful lie is better than an ugly truth!'

Because I believed them—your beautiful lies;

Beautiful like you and frigid like ice.

Scorned were countless, and the rest ignored away

But this time I thought I might stay.

For I remember the trust of the past;

This feeling of being loved at last!

Of a love so great, a glorious rain

That I felt it would actually remain.

Yet when the vernal storm did pass

I saw it for all it was;

A beautiful lie said to please,

One among the many said with ease.

The same lies, the same guys

But the difference lay in your eyes—

That when *you* said it,

I really believed it.

GONE

Holding withered flowers in vain,

Hoping they might bloom again.

Hiding this intense sea

Within the deepest core of me.

Surrounded by ashes of desire

That once burnt like fire,

Although my heart is still as true

As the *time* I vowed for you.

An unstoppable power, my soul's part,

Beating inside me like a second heart.

A lifetimes' worth of love, but to restrain

Consuming me to the utmost grain.

Gone—although I clutched at it

With all the hope of a heaven lit

And perhaps for the rest of my life blue,

This immense pain shall continue.

THE OTHER AND I

By the window frame, I watch the rain

While the Other watches the moon wane.

I see the gay November roses sway

While it sees tenuous petals wilt away.

I hear the wind toss to make music on boughs

While it hears the sad note as it goes.

I hold a pebble dewy white

Yet it notices only the scratches hidden from sight.

When convivial beings seek ties,

The Other notices the smiles failing to reach their eyes.

When I smile at the love in their heart

It frowns at the lust on their part.

But occasionally appear a few people, genuine,

With propitious intentions and less sin.

This time, it is they who flee from a helpless me

From the aloof walls, the Other has built to be

Wherein my heart shatters but *there*, the Other senses poetry blue;

Where I find empty parchments, it envisages words true.

Unwilling symbionts, together we walk by

The Other and I.

EVANESCING

So this is how stories fade;

With the mornings spent to forget

And the nights spent to remember

To look at you and think

'He used to be *mine*'.

Somewhere under the same sky

Breathing the same air as I

In this endless night

Even more *endless* in your absence.

Now I sit and count

The days we have been apart;

The days turning into weeks

The weeks turning into months

And the months slowly, into years...

And I wonder if I dreamt it all

Or how could I lose something,

Which wasn't *even* mine?

Indeed, rainbows are not

Meant to last

And embers will always

Die out in the end.

FLINTHEART

A desert with memories of rains that did part

Are the dark dregs of her abstruse heart

Surrounded by walls so steep

Where no fallacious bonds may creep.

Withered flowers, once in garish bloom

Adorn the graveyard of dream's doom.

For the glint in her eyes, of haunting art

Are of the stones that make her heart.

A hollow of secrets with shattered glass

Designed to deflect any unwelcome mass.

So do not be fooled by outward lustre phony

For her heart is cold, black and stony.

MOMENTS

Looking into those serene eyes

Twinkling like a thousand stars

Shimmering with love and depth,

I felt myself soar high.

Under the spell of a stare,

A million golden dreams I wove

And grew many a cherished hope;

Each one sweeter than the next.

Butterflies of eternity fluttered

In two hearts, too young

While feelings of blithe

Pranced in my soul.

Agony was it then, to tear my gaze away

From those calm eyes of deep meaning

Yet they took possession of my vision

Again and *again*.

And then, my heart beat faster,

My eyes twinkled with happiness,

A genuine smile lit my lips

For my whole world had just fallen together.

Outside, the moon had risen

And the stars came out.

Spring had arrived

For love just blossomed.

Tender, passionate and intense,

It had blossomed—

A feeling so beautiful, it would ache

Forever and longer.

ENAMORED

A million delightful dreams weaving magic,

Flamboyant flowers adorning a celestial reality

Fragrant songs of romance are sweeping me away

For with you, I have fallen in love.

Passion has laid its fingers on me

For you made the roses of resplendence bloom;

Every second seductive, every evening a fairy-tale,

Consummating the melody of my happy hopes.

Rain droplets of desire shower in my soul,

Gripped by a beguiling reverie.

Spilling spells, whisper of a warm wind

For the bells are chiming in my heart again.

WISTFUL WISH

I seek but an infinitesimal space in your heart

And fond remembrance each night before somnolence calls.

This inveigling risk I wish to take, want to make

For nights are longer now—though I cannot sleep—

With faint footsteps that invade my esoteric garden

Yet the child in me craves only beautiful lies to believe

And tender caresses to cherish eternally.

Though a game I play to lose

Shall it water the lilies in bloom?

Though these parochial stars may set

Will they light the cloud castle that I forged?

A space in your heart

That's all I ask.

INNER HAPPINESS

One day, depressed and forlorn,

Wishing to never have been born

Out stepped I, into the noon wood

Feeling anything but good.

The merry green was all around

And little blossoms grew on the ground;

Simple beauty, a simple vision—

Just the part of an afternoon session.

On I walked, quiet as ever

Perhaps with a little more fervour

As sweet chirping souls sought their fill

Flying overhead from beyond the hill.

Presently there flowed a river

Bubbling in exhilaration for the sunbeam, her lover.

Home to a million, a blue blessing,

Like a song, cheerfully flowing.

A mystical force, like a silent love

Made me look to the heavens above

Where yellow beams glowed with pure bliss

Enough to replace any sorrow with happiness.

Evening slowly set in,

As dazzling stars emerged without din.

The blue which was the sky's part

Seemed to me like the blue of my heart.

Yet as time went on

The golden moon rose in the night of lone

Shining, soothing, making me realize well

Everything the day had tried to tell.

Right there in the heart of nature, I

Was filled with a blissful sigh.

So near to God, no longer wry

I realized my inner smile would never die.

Because true happiness is one's own

None can steal, none could get it torn

And inwardly, once found

It remains forever bound.

THE END

Lonely are these remaining days

And frosty this forgotten fireplace.

I see a tired figure looking from the glass

With wrinkles, and strength that *was*.

The days are cold, so cold

And I grow sleepier and old.

Is it so soon ,winter lone?

It seems like only yesterday that it was dawn.

But it is evening already

With ghosts of undone deeds near me.

Only the tree I planted years ago remain

Its branches white like my hair does wane.

I wish I could fly plain

Like the peacocks want the rain.

I wish I could dance

Like the dreamers need the trance

But it is time grey

Like everybody has debts to pay.

And I can hear the wind bringing the Reaper Grim

Closer every second, seconds so dim…

COMPREHENSION

Injustice assailed like a cruel storm,

Causing my world to come crashing around me.

Where there used to be Success,

Remained broken pieces.

Dark days descended upon my wings.

Only the clock went on clicking

While problems continued to persist.

But somewhere in the midst of this wasted pile,

I found a light

That grew when I touched it.

Within this light was love

From the dregs of my cold soul.

There was faith sacred

That I had somehow missed for long.

There were simple joys

That my closed eyes could not see.

There were kith and kin

Shunned for worldly things.

So I broke the rigid rules and my heart grew.

I bowed my head and my angel spoke.

I forgave them all and my world shone.

Because in the end,

Happiness is a choice.

HEARTBREAKER

"Beware of him."

They repeat incessantly.

"For he drinks and does drugs."

The words echo.

But every time we talk

I half believe I'm the One.

"Watch out for his tricks."

Is indeed the general opinion

But can it be so wrong to think

Tricksters too, own a good side?

"Girls have come and gone to you"

It is so true.

"He is a heartbreaker, dear."

And quietly I do agree.

Yet when night falls

And half incoherent words flow

In a drunken stupor,

I know that this time

This heartbreaker has touched

Some part of my heart.

DISILLUSIONED

Perpetual like the lines on your hand

Sweeter than the shells on the sand

When a woman falls in love,

She *stays* in love.

Though she was slow to fall,

Her love will be long and whole.

Unlike hearts, that can change

And minds that waver as they age

Her love endures the thorns sown

By life upon the path dreary brown.

Men, though, take brief seconds to love

Like their love, which is only for *now*.

When the storm calms over the sea

Their hearts turn as cold as can be

With dwindling interest and voices sour

To a mystery that is no more.

But for all that can be said

Shadows always fade when led

And flames burn and die

Leaving behind only a silence, a sigh.

Such is the illusion of a romantic gleam

Easily broken, like a lost dream.

A WILFUL FANCY

Someday, years or months from now

Someday,

After seasons have come and gone,

When you hear a half whisper

Or the whisper of a whisper

Of my name,

I want the dregs of your soul

To quiver like pitiful branches

Shivering in the frost.

I want the strongest of storms

To rush in and wreck you

As you feel me like blood

Staining your hands

Staining all of yourself,

Rendering you unable to forget;

Unable to pretend I never happened.

ONCE MORE

Talk to me once more,

Like the old days have not gone sour.

Talk like they are still here

And the urge to sleep forever, I can bear.

Rejoice for the times good and bad

And sing, so that I may not be sad.

Dance like the days are still young to

And look at me once more, so that I may believe it too.

Laugh but one last laugh to ease

This pain, so that I may leave in peace.

The clock is ticking as I pray

Sleepy, so sleepy and grey…

WRONG GUY

Hardly the one I can take home

For players only love to play and roam.

Yet, when I look at you,

I realize 'opposites attract' to be true

So I close my ears to the warning ode

And get along this hazy road

Where you have been with so many dames

That you do not remember their names.

Because all those times wee

You said you loved me

You might have meant it

Just a little bit.

If there is white in every view

I want to see the white in you.

If there is an inch of goodness here

Then I want to touch it, dear.

And I wonder what it will cost me

To bring out the man I believe there to be.

A HANDFUL OF DREAMS

Arms laden with a sack of dreams, I stand

On this stifling road of stigma.

Alone and forsaken, with downcast eyes;

The jeers for mediocrity ringing in my ears.

But the rusty wire holding the rugged sack comes undone

And like branches, incandescent beams extend from within;

Specks of adoration glitter, stars of fame glint,

Lush leaves of lusty love start to swish.

A rainbow appears,

With a pot of exquisite coins at the far end

To wield a mighty sword

Whose steely blades shall extinguish the devils of yesterday

And quell the reasons for my inquietude

But reward the deserving beneficent,

The few companions

And nothing but a sardonic smirk

For the mockery that is now silent.

The sound of applause thunders,

As a smooth red carpet is drawn—

The carriage in wait, the onlookers a blur,

Flashes every second, debonair greetings every corner,

Festoons from the spectators,

And music in homage to me

As I drink in the infinite intoxication

Of a delightful calm.

Glory, finally, thwarted mind!

Recognition, at last, spurned heart!

As tawdry fireworks bedazzle

Awarding me my dreams,

Awarding me the whole wide world.

But all of a sudden, a furore intervenes

And a gong of debacle sounds.

The blossoms shrivel before my streaming eyes

The gems turn to stones, and

The masses but people who never believed.

'Poof', they vanish; holograms of some cruel magic,

Like little soap bubbles floating high—

Burst, oh, burst.

****

And in the end, I stand alone again,

A handful of dreams, all I ever had.

THE EX

As you wrap his heart

Around your little finger,

Holding it tethered

To cater to every whim and fancy,

All I can do is but wallow

In the grim, vain knowledge

That he was mine

Before he was ever yours.

As you put your arms

Around his narrow waist

Securing it tight

And bask in fondness

All I can do is but revel,

In the futile, dark satisfaction

That at least I did it first

Before you even knew him.

And as you and he

Weave silvery stories of laughter and love,

I seek solace in the aureate dreams

That he and I

Once dreamt and lost

For in those dreams I spent

A lifetime embracing his sweet love.

MOVING ON

I've cried my last tear;

Wounds don't mean pain,

Clouds don't mean rain

And *me* no longer means you.

This is how things fall apart,

This is why I've always said no.

Now the wasted fragments lying low

Are soon to be swept away.

Hard things have to be done,

Sad lives have to be lived

Because better days are only days away

And I can see what the skies say.

Each step was another mile,

Each pang was to be another smile.

Someday I hope you will be ripe enough

For the love, you could have had from me.

But did you think I'd wait forever?

Did you think I'd hang on longer?

This time, I'm leaving for good

And that's the way it will stay.

YOUR NAME

The pen falls to the paper

But this time

It is not words

I want to put down,

Not random ramblings not drifting hazes

That I wish to note,

But your name;

The pen writes by itself

Until all the ink has finished

And yet it continues

To trace *over* and *over*,

The letters

Of your name.

SCHIZOPHRENIC'S DESK

Like dreams within dreams made,

Realities appear and fade.

A summer dream here, a winter fall there

And moonlight from nowhere.

Like a candle in the breezy air

That it is how it is to be here nor there.

Eyes that exist, look on so

But I cannot speak the language they know.

A rain shower here, an autumn song there

Like vapours out of nowhere

While sober people stare

At my woven reality where

Pebbles loom and rainbows bloom

And fairylands of magic zoom.

Disembodied voices speak so near

Yet those closed ears do not hear.

But if the wind is invisible in our midst

Does it mean it does not exist?

Just because the eyes are shut to not see

Does everything else cease to be?

Shadows from invisible eyes follow;

Holograms or real? But away they go.

Yet those people from realities apart

See only my lone figure and a peculiar heart.

Dawns and dusks are but a trance

To awaken sometimes from this floating space.

Trails of paint on the canvas lie

Splashed in a frenzy, with a sigh.

Like a soap bubble in the air

That is how it is, to be in the middle of nowhere.

A spring season here, a hailstorm there

And the faintest of visions rare.

As like dreams within dreams made,

Realities appear and fade.

INEBRIATE

They smile at my smile

My smile that is a lie.

They rejoice at my joy

My joy that is a lie.

Some sneer because I have bowed,

Bowed so low that I cannot bow anymore.

Others applaud because I fight,

Fight so hard that nothing matters anymore.

But only a few remember to ask

About the pain that was.

Only a few wonder about the grief

That seems to be no more.

But I have buried it right here

Beneath flagons of wine, each night.

I have it buried within the intoxication

That neither love nor sleep can offer—

The blessed relief that carries me on

When all else has left me alone.

BOHEMIAN

I long to weave a silver dream

From the fairest star beam

When the mercurial tide so grand,

Rises high over the land.

I long to find faeries, beneath the skies

With resplendent wings and iridescent eyes

When a hush steals over the woods at night

Lulling it to slumber tight.

I long to seek remote lands with streams

That beckon in prescient dreams

For the world is a tangle of magick to me

Both perilous and pretty.

I long to tread with ease

Over the azure carpet of the seas

Until it meets the horizon blue

Inaccessible in its glory true.

I long to meet souls once known

As wanderlust drives me on;

Feverishly continuing to roam

For a place, I can finally call home.

I long for all

That I cannot have,

I long for so much

That I cannot explain.

I am the

Eternal gypsy,

The wanderer,

The one who *cannot* be tamed.

WINTER FALLS

When in Winter, the gelid winds blow

A phantasmagoria stirs in my heart, slow,

Re-awakening lovely memories while deluxe clouds lower

To adorn the grey horizon yonder

Shivering in the icy grip of a Winter fall.

When in Winter, glomerations of snow prance

Amidst the cerulean fog's dance,

Seeking the bare branches that stand forlorn;

A sapphire bloom in my heart's glen, is born

The blue of the ocean in its frozen core.

For when in Winter, the rains are true

And icicles gloss on somnolent buds blue,

A scintilla of love is in the air, and my bare soul

Making me one with this season whole

Inexplicably and inevitably.

Could it be that the chilly mist owns a part,

With its icy fingers, a bit of my heart?

SOUL-MATES

At twilight, the moonbeams fell

Upon my dark form cloaked in despair

As I gazed afar unseeingly

Beyond the smog of the mountains

And the grey of the remote sky.

You soared to appear then

As though from the horizon

While the black phantasm

That had gripped my life

Swiftly retreated with the wind.

Such was the might

Of this inexplicable magic.

Gratified were then,

The summer dreams which lay forgotten.

SHADOWS OF LIFE

A resplendent rejoicing

After centuries apart

As our intertwined souls

Whispered gentle spells

In a language unknown to all

With so much to share,

And too much to tell.

For even when the seas have turned to dust

And the blue rivers have dried,

My heart shall remain true to you—

The one who captured my lost heart.

FLORESCENCE

Behold the beauteous blossoms around

Although to silence they are bound

Enchanting and never wry—

Born in glory, and in glory, they die.

The Rose princess in a pink gown

Swaying amid the raindrops falling down,

Exudes a fragrant song of romance

With serenity and lustre in each dance.

The gentle Arum Lilly glows in white

Gracefully waltzing in delight

Like a comely bride in subtle wait

With chastity and without taint.

The gorgeous orchid in red

With valour and nobility to spread,

Sings passionately as it does blossom,

A song of desire, from its scarlet bosom.

The happy marigold that gleams in yellow

Prances with wealthy smiles so mellow

Like a carefree lass in the sun

With exhilaration rivalled by none.

The radiant violet in purple hue

Gazes in a trance so true,

Dreaming in the meandering breeze

As it emanates clemency and peace.

Reigning queens, together they make

The world a lovelier place in which to wake.

They remain, though so delicate,

Symbolic of many things intricate.

MERMAID SONG

I am a merry mermaid,

The sea's own fairy —

A part of the glorious ocean

And guardian of its

Splendorous waves.

Deep in the cyan depths,

I float and twirl

With my lustrous green mane

Swaying behind my speeding form

Amid fishes, oysters

And vibrant sea anemones.

On some idyllic evenings,

I pop my head out of the

Water sprinkled with foam

SHADOWS OF LIFE

To watch the mesmerizing sunset

On the distant horizon

Or later, to gaze at the silvery orb

Smiling down at me

From the velvet sky,

As the overwhelming silence all around

Pulses through the air.

Sometimes I dive swiftly

To the very bottom; the sea-bed

My violet eyes twinkling with mirth

Collecting pearls and exquisite stones

From long sunk ships;

Exploring the rare delights

Of my hidden,

Mystical universe.

On deserted, eerie nights, however,

I come out now and then

NAZREEN

From my resplendent blue world

On to the moonlit seashore

Beneath the shimmering stars

That beam, as though with pride,

To be entrusted with my secret,

And dance away like a blissful maiden

To the plaintive tune of the breeze —

Unseen and unheard

By the folks dwelling land.

THE DEPARTED SOUL

The rustling leaves enticed me

To bask in serene night beside the sea

But the whispering wind murmured of a loss—

A loss which lived and was.

The raindrops beckoned to frolic about

As plenty more remained in life to be sought

But eerie voices of many a ghost

Spoke sorrowfully of a soul lost.

Vague clouds led me on

To follow the trail of dawn

But the darkness kept reminding to mourn

An essence forever gone.

The stars and heavenly bodies above

Invited me to soar out and love

But the silence hindered, to remind

Of an everlasting sadness left behind.

FOREVER AND A DAY MORE

Staying up this lone night,

I listen to music loveliest;

That of his slumber tight.

Be still, my heart—

For I wish in vain

To hold him forever, and a day more.

In the hush that steals,

His breath away from my ear,

I see the starry skies linger

To play with me till I sing

The melody of our love

Forever, and a day more.

Lashes flutter faint, a murmur deep

As I trail my finger

Over lips that have

Taken me captive

With a love that I want

Forever, and a day more.

Within the sorcery of his silken form

Does he dream of me?

Be calm, my passion—

For here is a kiss across drifting moons

To cherish

Forever, and a day more.

PART 3

LIGHT OF MY LIFE

I love you like the lone little flower on the vast green field loves the rain. She waits all year and all day for the rain to pour, washing away everything—her happiness, sorrows, and trifles with it—until it merges with her soul, with the core of who she is, the very depth of her essence. I love you like that and in a hundred ways more. Because like the rain, everything sinks with you— me, my dreams, thoughts, desires and everything upheld close to my heart. They all sink like a hopeless little ship sinking in the deep ocean. Only they sink with a difference; the difference that is love.

Awake at night, sometimes whole nights on end, I lie under the starry skies, and the wind whispers to me about a faraway land waiting for the two of us. A perfect fairy-tale to envisage perhaps, but I've always said fairy-tales come true for those who believe in them. I'd fall asleep watching your perfect face, those lips which have taken me captive, and give into somnolence with the knowledge I'm *safe*; the one feeling I rarely have the luxury of feeling. Although I know dreams rarely come true, I want to dream this dream—dream, and dream—till every bit of reality crashes against this dream and it finally shatters into a million fragments.

Perhaps all that is going to remain in the end is the echo of our lovely love. Perhaps a few poems and prose more. Perhaps I will die solitary and embittered after all. I've trained my heart to let go of things that fly. Because somewhere inside, I am aware that the embers cannot spark forever and that they are bound to die out. But to feel this for you and for having you feel a tenth of this for me, that is enough for now. Some day they shall fade like all the rainbows that come and fade from our lives. For you do have the eyes of a person watching the sea. For even when I'm talking to you and you're talking to me, somebody within you always holds back from me and watches the whole scene warily.

But when twilight befalls the land, and the whole world is still, I realize it hasn't been quite this way before. For the rain gave the little flower life, and she, in turn, gave her love. Does the rain know of the intensity of her love, she who stands high and proud, one amongst the many pebbles on the mountain-top high? Does he understand the fierceness of the waiting she waits till he pours again, for he who made her bloom? Because if he did, he would never leave that highland meadow again. And that would disrupt the equilibrium of all things. For I am the little flower, and YOU, are the rain.

AFTERMATH

Some stories lose their charm—and ours lost *theirs* a very long time ago.

For I do not love you anymore, that is certain, and you have moved on and found happiness, that is irrefutable. It has been so long since when we first held hands, and even longer since we last held hands. Such that there is no more awkwardness when we sit beside each other and talk merrily, no more glimmer of remembering when our eyes meet across mobbed halls, no more trace of a shared history despite our shared laughter during gatherings, no more of anything to suggest we were once more than *whatever* we are now.

But sometimes, when the last of the cinders are sizzling in the fireplace hearth, I behold it and wonder why the bluebells in my heart leap when you walk into the room. Why sometimes my eyes gaze after your retreating shadow, why I am occasionally crestfallen when we are saying our goodbyes, and why I look *slightly* forward to the next time we might meet.

Though these whims pertaining to foregone times will never see the light of the day once more, sometimes I cannot help but wonder—Am I the only one who felt this way again?

CHOICE

They ask me to let go of you. They urge me to move on from what is no longer here. At the ends of their index fingers, across the shores that maroon me on this melancholy island, I can see creatures of gaiety shift in rhythm to festive lights and befuddling beats. I can see coruscating colours that have faded from where I am, and pleasures I have foregone since so long. And if only I could leave you and your waning memories, and go with them, then I can have everything I considered lost.

It shouldn't be too hard, really. Did they say it is difficult to embrace better things? Did anyone claim forgetting is not an easy task? In fact, it is easy to forget what is not pleasing to the mind, to let go of one person and flee to brighter shores. Anyone can give up on misery and continue forwards. Anyone can pretend it is all behind them now. Don't people do that all the time?

But what is hard is to stay here by myself and hold on to bygone whispers. What is hard is to pretend my hopes never fell in tatters. Although it is considered hard to let go, sometimes it is the other way around.

Because I have chosen to remain with your memories; without you. Not because I cannot leave you, but precisely because I *can*, and *will not*.

It is the choice of one who finds contentment in holding on to what we *were*.

QUESTION

There is a question—a dismal and dreadful one—that haunts you to no end as the darkest hour of a murky night befalls the land. When the last beam of daylight has faded away, it creeps along your bones, spreading its malicious tentacles to wreck your peace.

You relentlessly torture yourself with this question while several more questions arise from the focal one. Although you may have asked this countless times of your aggrieved self, you fail to attain any definite conclusion, or to reach anywhere with this needless misery that you carry.

But remember this—life has much more to offer than this one answer, much more beyond whatever this question limits or has come to limit. And sometimes this is all you need to bear in mind to set yourself free.

UNCHANGEABLE

You tell yourself you should have held on a little stronger or waited a little longer, but the truth is, this pain would still have come to pass.

You reproach yourself with endless regrets stemming from wayward thoughts, but no, this misfortune would still have happened in some form.

For what must happen, will happen.

And I hope when you realize this—realize this immutably and completely—you will finally be set *free*.

NAME

There is a name—that hurts your heart.

Like the remnant of some dreamy fable, out of place with all else, it has synchronized itself silently into the space between your inhales and exhales.

Echoing as though it had belonged there once, and at the same time, strange like it had never really fit in anywhere, sometimes you remember this name—and it hurts your heart.

FURY

They say some men use aggression to hide the tumult of emotions that rage within their hearts.

They say some of them conceal a love they cannot manage to suppress, behind the fury that flares up in their eyes.

I do not *know* if they are right, but oh, how I *hope*!

That your subtle displeasure might only be a sign you still care for me.

EXISTENCE

Standing there in the dusty corridor of your old school, among bygone ghosts of yesterday, you can see it vaguely — you have evolved, you have lived, and you have changed.

The faded classrooms look mildly a little too small, the playgrounds a little too old, and your heart seems just a little too hard. One way it all *looks* the same, but in another way it all *feels* very different. Time had come and swept you off with its smooth wings, and you perhaps did not realize until this day when you looked back and saw how much actually changed. And then it dawns on you that life itself had come and gone by while you were preoccupied with making everything better. It flew right over you while your mind was engrossed with a hundred things that do not seem very significant anymore.

But now, your white hair seems to glisten a little whiter and your vigour flicker to become a little less sharper. And you cannot help but evade the inevitable question—years or months, how much more time remains? How much time might be left to live once more—not just exist—but to be really *alive*?

PARADOX

They ask me if I am in love with you.

What answer do I give to this complicated question?

Let me count the paradoxes.

****

I do not wish to marry you, that is certain, for I am too much of myself to belong to anyone. But if I had to belong to anyone at all, then I cannot envision it to be one other than you.

It does not bother me too much that you do not love me, for the fancies of the heart may dwindle and kindle as it pleases. But then, if you were to love another, the limpid seas in my heart would storm and rage.

I do not really consider you much of a beauty or the sort that would wield poets imaginations and drive scores to a frenzy. And yet I often find that beauteous blossoms and winsome things pale in comparison to you.

When you walk by, I am hardly tempted to gaze at you with eyes they tell me are like azure lakes of glass, but if you did not walk by at all, then the chill of a dead winter would grip my bones.

I often ignore your presence, although its incandescence can be hard to miss, but if you were to be absent from there, then even one hundred people could not make the room lively.

I do not spin daydreams of bliss and blithe around you, for the world is large and its pleasures are many. But the aftermath of an occasional nightmare is often soothed by embracing thoughts of you.

****

What is this feeling? The one they call love?

If it is, then what name do I name this strange kind of love?

And in ignorance, those simple people still ask me this very complicated question to which the answers are long and large.

NOTHINGNESS

As you remember how you were betrayed, as you replay how everything fell into pieces one by one, you don't just feel sad or angry. Because grief and anger can be endured, and I know you have trained your heart to get used to the hurt that is inevitable with love.

But this didn't just change the way you thought about love, this isn't just about a shattered illusion of romance. Instead, it is like all your dreams, thoughts, ideals, who you are and the way you loved and cherished yourself was taken from you, crushed into a huge worthless ball and powdered into dust and nothingness.

Although this makes it seem harder to recover, ultimately — like an intricate paradox—it will also make it easier to heal. Remember, it was from nothingness that new things came into being, and into nothingness that they eventually disappear. If this is the end of one thing, it is also the beginning of another. And there is a beautiful new dawn lurking behind the tears of that bleak cloud, waiting for the day you will embrace it whole-heartedly.

INCOMPATIBLE

You could serenade me on the placid evenings and etch evocative poems on idyllic nights but it would *all* go away at the first trace of dawn.

You can pretend to be the blue of my ocean and the green in my meadow but *still* will fade away when the wintry fog starts to descend.

Everything you did, was never enough.

Anything you might be willing to do, will also never be enough.

For all the light of the stars in heaven will not lend spark,

To a love, that is just not *meant to be.*

IF ONLY

If only the bygone days when your eyes were still sparkling for me, would return, I would put all these wrongs to right.

If only those hours when you used to write my name all over your books, would return, I would crush your letters close to my heart.

If only the foregone moments when we whispered over every rose that bloomed, would return, I would cherish each and every word that ever fell from your lips.

If only those dawns when you lay awake thinking about me, would return, I would hold you like I'd never let go again.

If only the nights when I wove in and out of your dreams, would return, I would paint them all with the most resplendent of hues.

If only the scorching summers would return, I would wipe every invisible tear I failed to see, and stand by your silence knowing it was all you had to offer then.

If only, *if only*... Time would recede and you were mine again, I would hold on, look past the imperfections, and love you the way I should have loved you.

FALLOUT

You know how it is. You think you have healed from the haunting and got past what tormented you, as you go on resolutely, braced to face any more stones hurled your way. The mark of a survivor shines out of every fibre of your being. But then one fine, sunny morning—that glistens with tranquillity as though nothing could ever go wrong that day—you wake up and everything rushes back into your head; the fear, the guilt, the horror of it all.

It then feels like all the previous months of recovering wasn't ever real. Like all the times you almost gave up but persevered on to *fight and fight*, never happened at all. The meticulous work put into getting better suddenly seems to have been wasted because this isn't what you were working towards; this break-down in the middle of nowhere. It will seem like there is no light to be found, no bright place to escape into, as an endless stretch of hopelessness pervades your senses.

Know that it is only a matter of looking hard enough, because undoubtedly, somewhere in the dark mess you think you are, there IS an escape lurking. On days that appear like everything is back to where it started, remind yourself of the mountains you conquered, and the strength you were rewarded with after each climb. Nothing can snatch it away from you now, and these weak imitations of darkness will pale before the absolute strength in your determined self.

The healing STARTS and ENDS with you after all.

INTERTWINED

I know it, *inexplicably*, when you think about me.

When the glimmer of a memory of me flits across your mind, I can feel it thudding in my chest.

In that moment, no matter what task I am engaged in, or whatever convoluted thoughts might be enthralling my attention, my soul shivers like it has stepped into an icy shower, and my breath catches for a second.

As though the wind had whispered this lovely secret into my ear, I stiffen and shine, knowing somewhere, somehow; YOU had thought about me.

BETRAYAL

There is this pain in my heart—this pain that is so intense and silently poetic that it blends within the blue of my soul and sometimes I forget that it even exists.

But it is there, it is *always* there.

Like the breeze that caresses the branches on a still night, like the dim stars on a dusky sky, like the words that adorn a verbose mind. The pain—if it can be called a pain at all—that stems from your betrayal.

NAZREEN

ABOUT THE AUTHOR

Nazreen is a doctor by day and a poet by night (and somewhere in the middle during afternoons and evenings). As a child who wished to alter the conclusions of several fairy-tales, she gradually started fabricating her own fables and later with the passing of years, latched on to poetry, prose and short stories.

When not writing or away at work, she can be found meditating, tending to the garden or feeding stray cats.

She currently resides in the Middle East with her family.

To read more, connect with her on social media platforms:
Instagram.com/dr.nazreen
Twitter @dr_nazreen_

Printed in Great Britain
by Amazon